CHINA 1980

PICTURES FROM ANOTHER ERA

MIKE EMERY

EARNSHAW BOOKS

China 1980
by Mike Emery

ISBN-13: 978-988-8769-97-1

HISTORY / Asia / China

EB179

Published in Hong Kong by Earnshaw Books Ltd.

Iwas a photographer aboard one of the first ever American passenger cruise ships sailing the China coast. It was 1980 and nobody on board had ever been to China. It was a whole new experience filled with great excitement. China was, at the time, a seldom travelled-to country for Westerners. It was a period of rapid change and excitement, with economic and cultural reforms sweeping the country.

It has been more than forty years since I captured this rare collection of street photographs, and much has changed in the years since. So it's definitely time for these images to be shared to the world.

This book features images that almost seem to be from another world. Many of those whose images are recorded here are children, and I have often wondered what happened to them, where they are today, how their lives have changed in the decades since I fleetingly interacted with them and I was lucky enough to witness them open up their hearts to me.

The images were shot on Nikon cameras with a variety of lenses and Metz and Braun flash guns using color negative film as well Kodachrome transparency film. Pre auto focus and digital cameras, it was at times, by today's standards, a challenge to get the shots I wanted. Everything was manual and the exposure was set and focused by hand.

When our ship first docked at the port city of Tientsin
(Tianjin), we didn't know what to expect, but it was like
a carnival. There was an air of excitement, complete with
flags, streamers and a marching band to greet us.

I stood out — this foreigner with fair hair carrying a
strange object (my Nikon) and wearing colorful clothes — a
rare sight to behold on an adult in China at that time.

Most people I met had never seen such a camera before,
nor did they know what to do when one was pointed at
them. They were completely fascinated. I am not easily
embarrassed. I pulled funny faces, stuck my tongue out
or lay on my back in the middle of the street, trying to
stimulate some kind of reaction.

Groups of up to fifty people would surround me,
wanting to speak English, all supremely curious. They
were all invariably polite and would ask, "Excuse me,
may I practice my English?"

During successive trips to China, I observed and
captured changes in the general appearance of Chinese
society. People started to become more individual,
expressing themselves with new clothes and more
adventurous hair styles. Luxury goods such as black
and white TVs started to appear in the shop windows in
Shanghai. You had a feeling that change was on the horizon
with rise of billboard advertising along with slogans from
Chairman Mao.

Long after my cruise ship days had ended, I realised the
significance of the street photos that I had captured during
those trips to China. There are very few photographs
available from that period dedicated to people going
about their daily lives.

What seems to unite the people on these pages, from my outside and possibly naïve perspective, is a feeling of contentment. When you look at the laughing faces of these children, you can see the innocence in their eyes. There is no sense of stress, life was simple. Pure happiness seems to erupt from the smiles of these beautiful people.

In 1980, housing in China's cities was extremely scarce with much overcrowding. The population was growing, many families lived in single-storey housing compounds, with several generations occupying the same confined space. Luxuries were for the future. There were few TVs, no internet, no motor cars parked in the driveway. Bicycles were kept inside as they were considered a valuable luxury.

Children make up a large part of this book. They are wonderful subjects to photograph and their character shines through these pages. You will see their cheekiness, their joyfulness and the way their stance evokes a sense of pride, both personal and cultural.

It is also significant to note that the late 1970s marked the beginning of the country's one-child policy, abandoned only recently. You will notice in the pictures that children everywhere are dressed in brightly coloured clothes, a distinct difference to the shades of blue, brown and khaki then worn by their parents and elders.

They did not know it, but they were on the verge of a complete change in the trappings of life, more Westernised in many ways and a far cry from what their parents were used to.

I also have a vast appreciation for how strong the family bonds were, the integration of the generations with grandparents and grandchildren so often together.

The pace of life in China's cities in 1980, as I observed it, was steady. There was a calmness that was foreign to me. The bicycles weaved along the streets, and the buses meandered slowly. There was no hustle and bustle or sense of rush hour.

I hope this journey through the streets of Shanghai and Beijing provides an insight into Chinese society as it was in 1980, and, by comparison, appreciate how much it has changed since.

I've spent many years wondering where the children on the pages of this book are now. The girl in uniform standing standing proudly in Tiananmen square. The cheeky little chap biting into an apple. What did they go and accomplish? The beaming youth on the pages are now middle aged and elders. It would be so fulfilling to know what became of their lives.

Do you know them? Where are they now?

Can we find them?

CHINA 1980

Inquisitive faces around a food vendor.

SHANGHAI
1980

Young people passing the time playing cards.

SHANGHAI
1980

A little boy on a bus fascinated by my camera.

BEIJING
1980

A family outing in the Forbidden City.

BEIJING
1980

Helping in the fields, getting a great reaction from the ladies.

BEIJING
1980

A family group photo.

SHANGHAI
1980

Young children in Tiananmen Square with their teachers.
They look mature with caps and head scarfs.

BEIJING
1980

*A young man
selling fish.*

SHANGHAI
1980

Family at the Beijing train station.

BEIJING
1980

Mother and daughter

11

Chinese people dress their children in bright colors.

SHANGHAI
1980

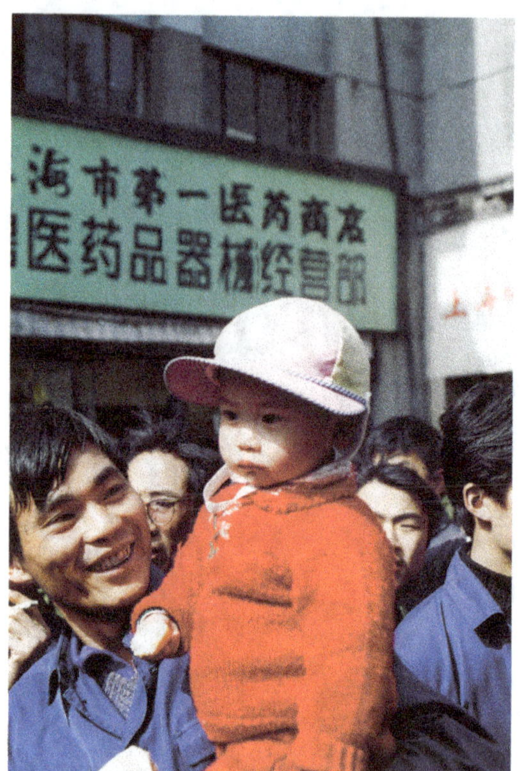

Chinese parents swap around babysitting duties.

SHANGHAI
1980

12

Father with two young boys in the Forbidden City.

BEIJING
1980

The noticeable closeness of Chinese families.

SHANGHAI
1980

14

Grandmother looking after a
little girl with an ice block.

BEIJING
1980

15

A mother knitting her daughter a hat.

Father with his little girl.

BEIJING
1980

16

Children on their way to school.

SHANGHAI
1980

Three official looking gentlemen on a motorbike.

BEIJING
1980

18

Children singing and dancing at a kindergarten.

BEIJING
1980

Families arriving by train.

BEIJING TRAIN STATION
1980

Photographer with children in Tiananmen Square.

BEIJING
1980

Children at a kindergarten.

BEIJING
1980

22

Three ladies knitting colorful clothes for their children.

BEIJING
1980

A fashionable young lady with rosy cheeks and maybe a splash of makeup.

BEIJING
1980

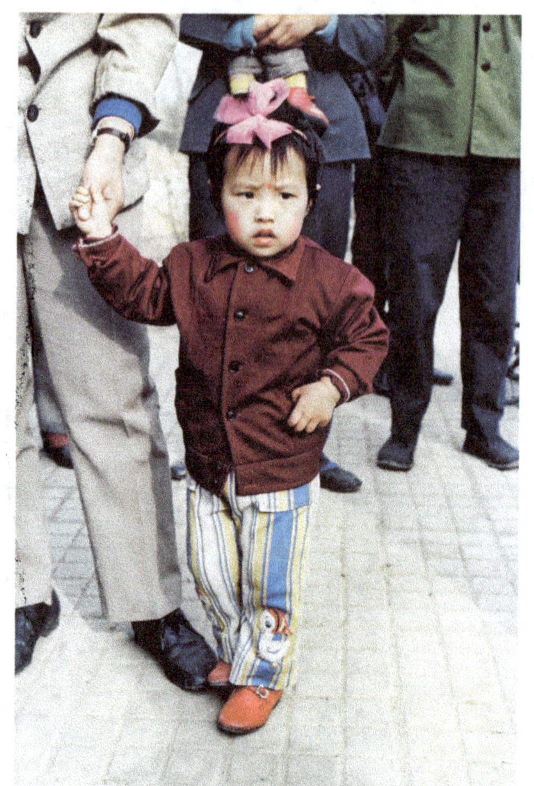

Brother and sister.

SHANGHAI
1980

24

*The boys are wearing blue and green military-style caps
with red stars.*

BEIJING
1980

A shipyard on the Huangpu River.

SHANGHAI
1980

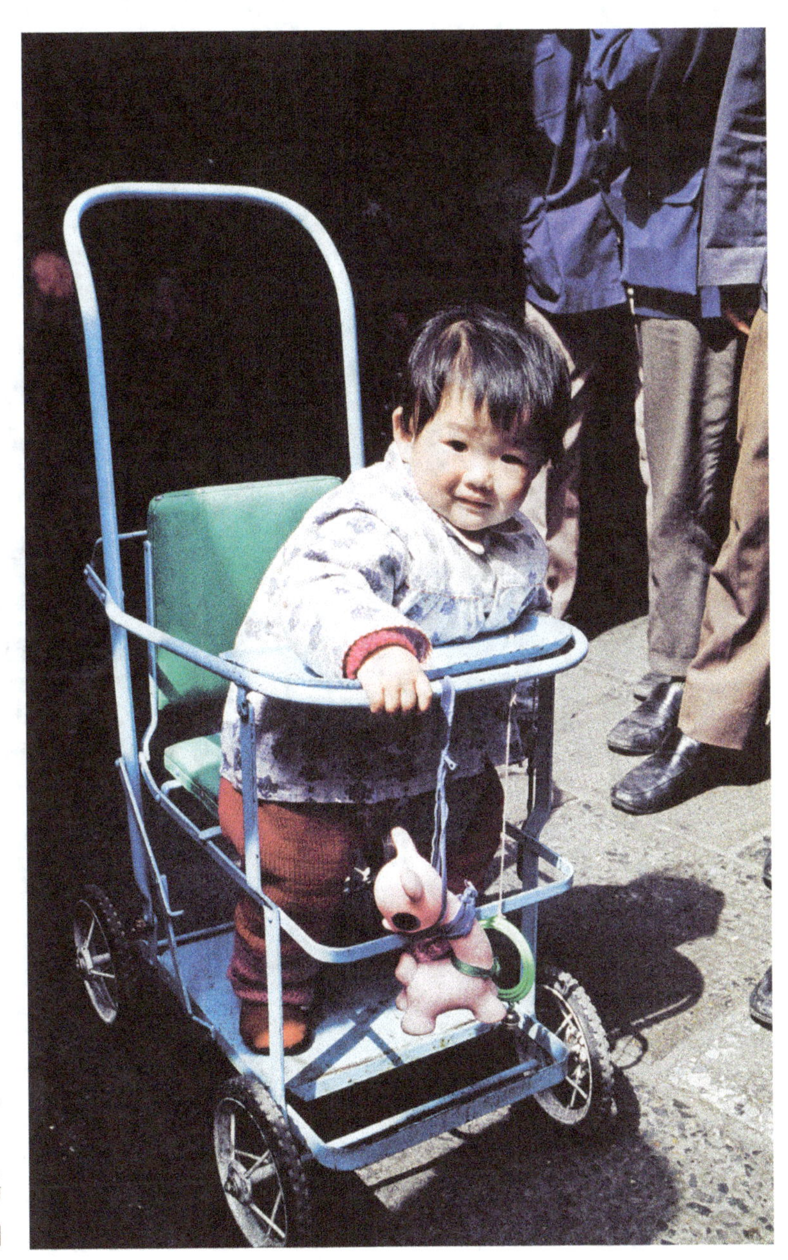

Baby in stroller.

BEIJING
1980

Pre-school children enjoying a day out at Tiananmen Square.

BEIJING
1980

28

"All very serious." Older boys wearing blue / grey / beige uniforms.

BEIJING
1980

*A little boy holding chewing gum and an apple given
to him by a passenger from the ship.*

BEIJING
1980

Little girl in pink with a blue handbag.

BEIJING
1980

One of my favorite photographs. He wanted me to hold him. Temple of Heaven.

BEIJING
1980

32

Two shy girls in a street market.

SHANGHAI
1980

Beautiful old buildings in the Forbidden City.

BEIJING
1980

*Little boy with a
new bike.*

BEIJING
1980

A little girl holding very tight to her father.
Note her stylish bag.

SHANGHAI
1980

Little boy with a red necktie.

BEIJING
1980

*Two young boys,
one with a toy
gun.*

BEIJING
1980

Young children in Tiananmen Square holding hands,
a few funny faces.

BEIJING
1980

Smiling faces.

BEIJING
1980

Children with colorful clothes and beautiful expressions.

BEIJING
1980

Young girls playing a hand game.

BEIJING SUMMER PALACE
1980

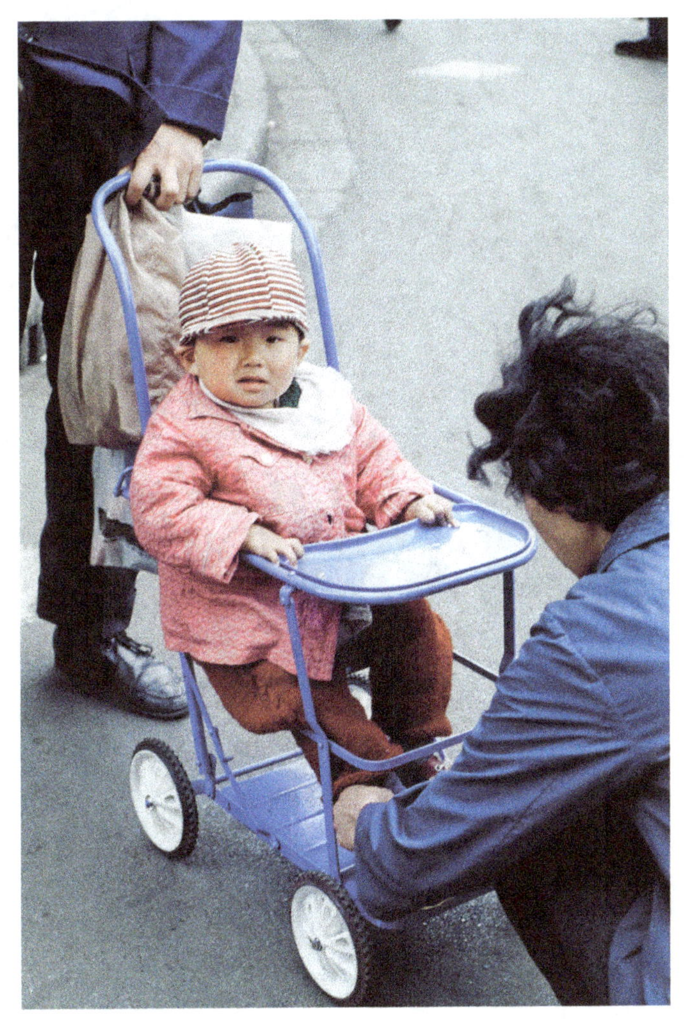

Little girl riding in a new stroller.

SHANGHAI
1980

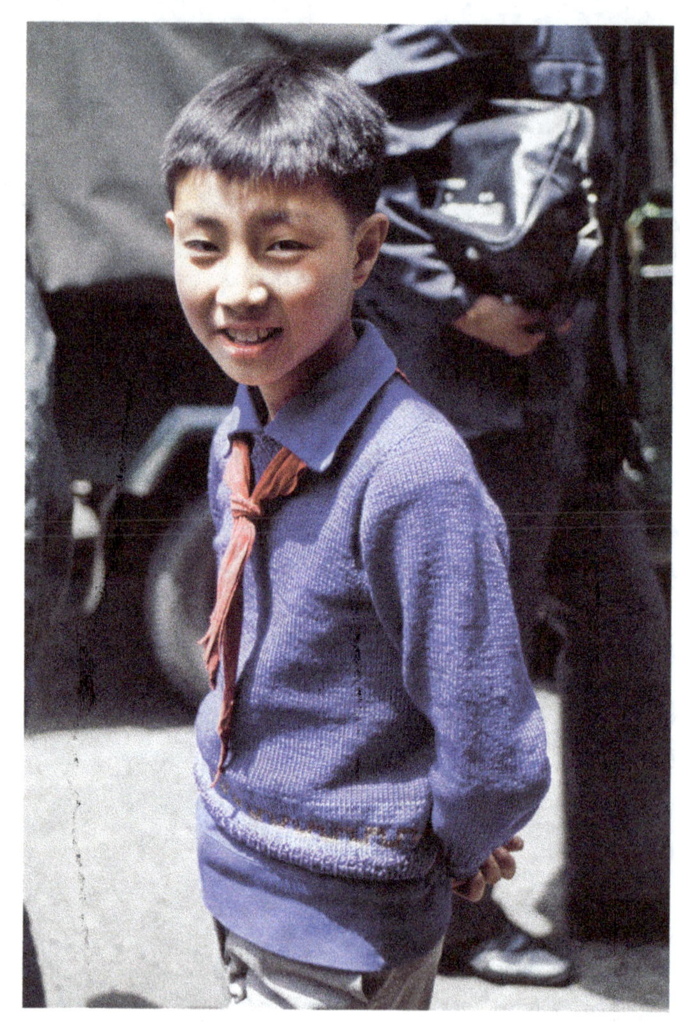

Confident young boy with a red necktie.

BEIJING
1980

Little boy balanced on his father's bike.
There is a reflection of me on the silver bell.

BEIJING
1980

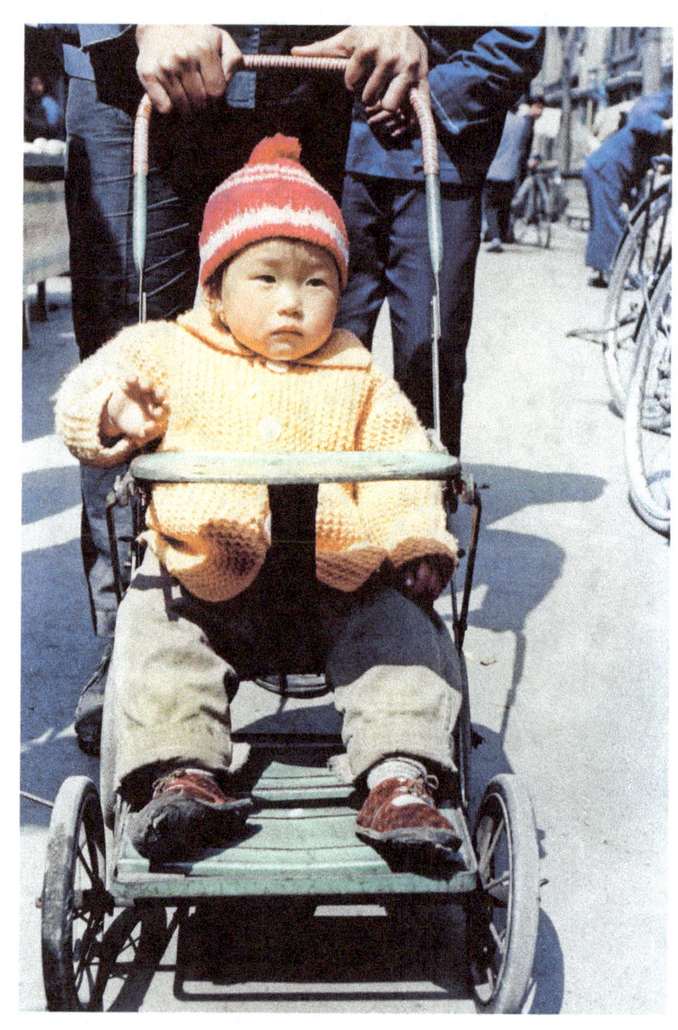

A well-worn push chair, colorful clothes.

SHANGHAI
1980

A nice hat to keep the ears warm.

BEIJING
1980

*A happy girl.
I put up my
thumb and she
copied me.*

BEIJING
1980

*Young boys outside the Great Hall of the People,
well-prepared with shoulder bags and water bottles.*

BEIJING
1980

Little girl in the Summer Palace holding a flag.

BEIJING
1980

These children at the Summer Palace wanted to do a group shot for the passengers on our ship.

BEIJING
1980

*Happy young
girl posing with
a ceremonial
lions at the
Summer Palace.*

BEIJING
1980

52

… and her brother wanting to get into the action.

BEIJING
1980

Beautiful expression. He's not sure about me.

BEIJING
1980

Group of young children clapping and singing in Tiananmen Square.

BEIJING
1980

*School children visiting the Monument to
the People's Heroes.*

BEIJING
1980

Little boy in a red cap.

SHANGHAI
1980

A shy boy.

BEIJING
1980

Hand-made cart for a little boy.

SHANGHAI
1980

*Older brother looking after younger brother with
mother in the background.*

BEIJING
1980

Large group of school children, out for the day in the Summer Palace. On the left is a man with a camera, a rare sight in those days.

BEIJING
1980

*I was making
these young
children laugh
in Tiananmen
Square.*

BEIJING
1980

So many beautiful children's faces on Tiananmen Square.

BEIJING
1980

Group of school children.
Outskirts of Beijing

BEIJING
1980

64

Twin girls with balloons in the Forbidden City. One little girl holds an empty Kodak film box. They were the only twins I saw in China.

BEIJING
1980

65

This little boy looks very grown up with
his cap on his head.

BEIJING
1980

Little girl with a bright red jacket and hair in pigtails.

BEIJING, FORBIDDEN CITY
1980

*School
children at
a parade in
Tiananmen
Square.*

BEIJING
1980

68

Young boys looking well-disciplined in Tiananmen Square.

BEIJING
1980

Young boy on his way to school, holding his mug.

SHANGHAI
1980

Ice blocks like these were a favorite with the children.

BEIJING
1980

A little girl dressed in pink, eating an apple.

BEIJING
1980

Children dancing at a kindergarten with chicken hats.

OUTSKIRTS OF BEIJING
1980

Singing! At the kindergarten.

BEIJING
1980

74

Children with their musical instruments ready to play.

BEIJING
1980

Older children dancing, wearing colorful costumes.

BEIJING
1980

Pretty young children.

BEIJING
1980

Little boy with oversized hat.

BEIJING
1980

A little girl holding a bun.

SHANGHAI
1980

Little boy with a naval hat.

SHANGHAI
1980

Home-made stroller.

SHANGHAI
1980

A little boy, well, he looks like a little man…

BEIJING
1980

82

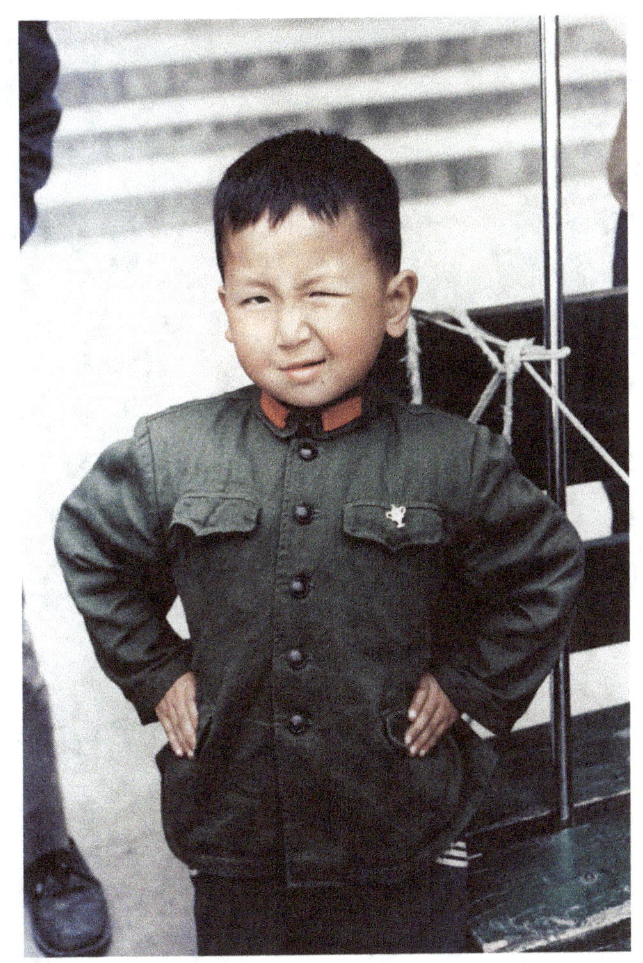

Little boy winking at me, after I showed him how it was done.

BEIJING
1980

Little boy and girl at the Summer Palace.

BEIJING
1980

84

Young boy, at the Summer Palace.

BEIJING
1980

Group of young children in Tiananmen Square.

BEIJING
1980

Little boy giving me a wave.

BEIJING
1980

*Young boy with balloon, wandering around
the Forbidden City.*

BEIJING
1980

*Young guys taking a break, dressed
in their work clothes.*

SHANGHAI
1980

Workers on the streets of Shanghai, curious at being photographed.

SHANGHAI
1980

A school outing to Tiananmen Square.

BEIJING
1980

*Hundreds of children lining up to see visit Mao's Mausoleum,
the vastness of Tiananmen Square in the background.*

BEIJING
1980

Three young boys.

BEIJING
1980

Young boy, lunch over.

SHANGHAI
1980

Young girls experimenting with colorful clothes and changes to their hairstyles.

BEIJING
1980

Young workers in heavy clothing in the Forbidden City.

BEIJING
1980

96

Strong young lady in Tiananmen Square, beautiful face, leader of the group.

BEIJING
1980

*A young man
proudly holding
a flag at a
youth parade
in Tiananmen
Square.*

BEIJING
1980

Young people paying their respects to revolutionary martyrs on Tiananmen Square. In the background is the Great Hall of the People.

BEIJING
1980

*A young lady addressing her schoolmates in
Tiananmen Square.*

BEIJING
1980

Happy children in Tiananmen Square.

BEIJING
1980

Children in Tiananmen Square laying a wreath
at the Monument of the People's Martyrs.

BEIJING
1980

Young man strolling through the Forbidden City.

BEIJING
1980

Ladies watching the passing scene.

BEIJING
1980

104

Older gentleman reading the newspaper.

SHANGHAI
1980

One of the few luxuries I saw in China, a radio!

SHANGHAI
1980

Women engaging in their favorite pastime, knitting.

BEIJING
1980

A traditional Chinese pipe in the Forbidden City.

BEIJING
1980

108

*The elderly were constantly doing chores. There was
no internal water supply in most Chinese homes,
and water came from communal taps.*

BEIJING
1980

*Two elderly people outside their modest home,
dressed in standard blue garb.*

BEIJING
1980

110

She is wearing a pair of earrings, which was unusual.

BEIJING
1980

*Older gentleman
with a great
beard.*

BEIJING
1980

112

Clothes hung out to dry by a small house with two elderly people passing the time of day.

SHANGHAI
1980

113

*Lady doing
washing at the
communal tap.*

BEIJING
1980

114

Early morning exercises outside the Friendship Hotel in Beijing.

BEIJING
1980

Lady with beautifully charactered face.

BEIJING
1980

Workman in the Forbidden City wearing
several layers of clothes holding a cigarette

BEIJING
1980

Shoes were constantly re-soled.
This man is very happy in his work.

BEIJING
1980

A man splitting bamboo probably to make baskets.

BEIJING
1980

Working in the fields in the suburbs of the capital.

BEIJING
1980

120

A man weaving cotton. Plenty of movement in this photo.

BEIJING
1980

*Men and women
work together on
construction sites.*

BEIJING
1980

122

Carpenter busy at work.

BEIJING
1980

No sign of construction machinery, all labour done by hand.

BEIJING
1980

124

*Ladies working in the fields wearing hats to ward off
the sun on the capital's outskirts.*

BEIJING
1980

Traditional Chinese painting at a cultural workshop.

BEIJING
1980

126

Art item production at a cultural workshop.

BEIJING
1980

Tractor cart, carrying mud.

BEIJING
1980

Ready steady go, the race is on. Bicycles were a major form of transport.

SHANGHAI
1980

Bicycles and more bicycles.

SHANGHAI
1980

130

Transport in the capital. Wide roads, small mini-van buses, very few traffic lights so policemen stood on little pedestals to direct the traffic.

BEIJING
1980

131

A lady carrying a big load on the back of her tricycle cart.

SHANGHAI
1980

132

A man giving his wife a ride on the back of his bicycle.

SHANGHAI
1980

Lady street cleaner on Nanjing Road with an electric bus in the background.

SHANGHAI
1980

A bendy bus crosses an intersection in the capital.

BEIJING
1980

*An elderly gentleman pushing his tricycle cart
in the Forbidden City.*

BEIJING
1980

136

Motorcyclist postman giving me a wave.

BEIJING
1980

Street scene outside a restaurant.

BEIJING
1980

A barge transporting freight on the Yangtze River.

SHANGHAI
1980

Ferry filled with people crossing the Yangtze River.

SHANGHAI
1980

An old junk on Huangpu River.
Note the crew's washing strung out on the deck.

SHANGHAI
1980

*Shipbuilding yard on the Pudong side of the
Huangpu River.*

SHANGHAI
1980

Tug boat on the Huangpu River.

SHANGHAI
1980

Boat full of Chinese tourists at the Summer Palace.

BEIJING
1980

144

Everyone wants to fix the truck.

BEIJING

1980

145

*Traffic jam at
the Great Wall.*

BEIJING
1980

146

A ferry on the Huangpu River.

SHANGHAI
1980

An industrial area on the Huangpu River.

SHANGHAI
1980

Cycling to work past two-story worker accommodation.

BEIJING
1980

*A cyclist with
a child carriage
attachment.*

SHANGHAI
1980

150

Rows of bicycles. How would you know which was yours?

BEIJING
1980

*A cyclist on his
way to work.*

BEIJING
1980

152

Street life on Nanjing Road.

SHANGHAI
1980

A Chinese cargo junk on the Huangpu River.

SHANGHAI
1980

154

Various ships and boats on the Huangpu River.

SHANGHAI
1980

Shopping day, ladies wandering around with shopping bags.
Two horses busy eating the hay.

SHANGHAI
1980

Official motorbike and sidecar on patrol.

BEIJING
1980

157

Horse and cart carrying goods to market.

BEIJING
1980

Shipping in Shanghai, looks like a ferry in the foreground.

SHANGHAI
1980

160

Huangpu River. Various boats.

SHANGHAI
1980

Friendly lady selling tickets at the Temple of Heaven.

BEIJING
1980

A happy young butcher says hi.

SHANGHAI
1980

163

Fish for sale — street sellers and customers.

SHANGHAI
1980

*A worker weighs
out eggs in front
of a shop.*

SHANGHAI
1980

165

A little girl and her mother shopping for food at an open-air market.

SHANGHAI
1980

166

*Ladies selling food at a street market – mushrooms with
pieces of pork.*

SHANGHAI
1980

A street vendor serving food to a policeman.

SHANGHAI
1980

168

Selling freshly made noodles.

SHANGHAI
1980

A proud mechanic happy to be photographed.

BEIJING
1980

A normal street in China's biggest city, not a car in sight.

SHANGHAI
1980

A solitary man crossing the road before the rush of bikes descends.

BEIJING
1980

An egg seller.

SHANGHAI
1980

Bicycles and people, deeply uniform.

SHANGHAI
1980

A masked face in a crowd.

SHANGHAI
1980

Busy street filled with sellers and buyers.

SHANGHAI
1980

School outing to
Tiananmen Square.

BEIJING
1980

A frozen lake with the marble boat at the Summer Palace.

BEIJING
1980

178

One of the many beautiful buildings in the Forbidden City.

BEIJING
1980

A man on a bicycle riding past the gate of
a government office compound.

BEIJING
1980

180

Shoppers outside two stores, a bookstore
and a photographic studio.

SHANGHAI
1980

Family members outside their home. The young man holding a mug with chopsticks inside.

BEIJING
1980

182

*Wide streets with one lane for bicycles and
one for cars and trucks.*

SHANGHAI
1980

183

A policeman on a bicycle with a movie billboard in the background.

SHANGHAI
1980

A small store on the outskirts of the city.

BEIJING
1980

The Great Wall, a favorite place for people to visit.

BEIJING
1980

Beautiful buildings in the Forbidden City.

BEIJING
1980

Frozen lake at the Summer Palace in the late afternoon.

BEIJING
1980

*Workers re-painting a beautiful ornate building
in the Forbidden City*

BEIJING
1980

The Forbidden City.

BEIJING
1980

The backyard of a small house, with grandma looking
after a child.

BEIJING
1980

A store selling baskets and wooden brooms.

BEIJING
1980

192

The Summer Palace lake in spring.

BEIJING
1980

193

Our ship's hairdresser roller skating on the Waibaidu Bridge. The locals were fascinated.

SHANGHAI
1980

194

A cold but sunny day on the Great Wall.

BEIJING
1980

A curious young girl.

BEIJING
1980

196

The Great Wall.

BEIJING
1980

*The snake-like
Great Wall with
a rare foreigner
in view.*

BEIJING
1980

198

Photographer and children in Tiananmen Square.

BEIJING
1980

*A winter's day in the Forbidden City, a dusting of snow
on the ground.*

BEIJING
1980

Young worker taking a break.

SHANGHAI
1980

*Proud grandma, encouraged me to take
a photograph.*

BEIJING
1980

202

Young man not sure about me.

SHANGHAI
1980

My favorite workers laughing as I take their photo.

BEIJING
1980

Beautiful faces, kids all dressed in colorful outfits.

BEIJING
1980

Cheeky faces outside a kindergarten.

BEIJING
1980

*Young man
walking home
from work.*

BEIJING
1980

Bikes, buses and cars on the capital's main thoroughfare.

BEIJING
1980

208

A street sweeper, and some stylish young ladies.

BEIJING
1980

School children having a great time on the marble boat at the Summer Palace.

BEIJING
1980

I don't think he wanted me to take his photo.

BEIJING
1980

The Summer Palace.

BEIJING
1980

*Father and his two boys having a great day inside
the Forbidden City.*

BEIJING
1980

213

*Happy faces while in the background a man climbs
on a lion to be photographed.*

BEIJING
1980

An elderly man doing exercises on a grey morning.

BEIJING
1980

*Young lady painting a beautiful picture
at a cultural workshop.*

BEIJING
1980

A lady doing stretching exercises.

BEIJING
1980

*Children in Tiananmen Square paying their respects to
fallen soldiers.*

BEIJING
1980

*A young man taking his partner for a ride
on his bicycle.*

BEIJING
1980

ABOUT THE AUTHOR

Mike Emery was born in Stoke-on-Trent, Staffordshire, England. He went to various local schools before doing a diploma of education in visual arts and communications which it included photography.

He then went on to do a professional photography course with the ultimate aim of working on cruise ships as a photographer. Knowing this would prove a challenge, he spent his nights learning to be a croupier to have another string to add to his bow.

Mike was lucky enough to get a job on a new cruise ship based in Japan heading in to China. By day and early night he photographed the passengers. Later that night he opened the casino on-board where he dealt blackjack.

He stayed on various cruise ships traveling the world for several years.

Eventually Mike settled down and got married in Sydney Australia, where he started a wedding and portrait business until the early nineties. It was then that he could see a need for real estate photography, so he built a business specializing in this which has taken him up to the present day.

Mike feels he has been very lucky to be a photographer and to make a living doing what he enjoys.